WHO TRAVELLED THE UNDERGROUND RAILROAD?

Cath Senker

raintree
a Capstone company — publishers for children

Raintree is an imprint of Capstone Global
Library Limited, a company incorporated
in England and Wales having its registered
office at 7 Pilgrim Street, London, EC4V 6LB
– Registered company number: 6695582

www.raintreepublishers.co.uk
myorders@raintreepublishers.co.uk

Edited by Andrew Farrow, Patrick Catel, and
  Vaarunika Dharmapala
Designed by Steve Mead
Original illustrations © Capstone Global
  Library Ltd 2014
Illustrated by HL Studios
Picture research by Ruth Blair
Originated by Capstone Global Library Ltd
Printed in China

ISBN 978 1 406 27309 0 (hardback)
17 16 15 14 13
10 9 8 7 6 5 4 3 2 1

ISBN 978 1 406 27316 8 (paperback)
18 17 16 15 14
10 9 8 7 6 5 4 3 2 1

**British Library Cataloguing in Publication
Data**
Senker, Cath
Who travelled the Underground Railroad?
(Primary source detectives)
A full catalogue record for this book is
available from the British Library.

Acknowledgements
We would like to thank the following for
permission to reproduce photographs:
Alamy pp. 32 (© Tom Uhlman), 48 (© Everett
Collection Historical); Corbis pp. 4 & 25
(© Bettmann), 50 (© Reuters); © Corbis
pp. 13, 20; CRIA Images p. 45 (Jay Robert
Nash Collection); Getty Images pp. 15
(Jerry Pinkney/National Geographic), 18
(Jupiterimages), 28 (Stock Montage), 47
(Chicago History Museum), 55 (MPI), 56
(Time & Life Pictures); Library of Congress
p. 16; Mary Evans pp. 26, 39; Superstock
pp. 37 (ClassicStock.com), 41 (Universal
Images Group), 52 (Culver Pictures, Inc.);
Topfoto pp. 9 & 10 (The Granger Collection),
23 (Topham Picturepoint); Wikipedia pp. 14
(NYU FC 2), 34 (Matt H. Wade), 43 (source
unknown).

Cover photograph of a slave family in cotton
fields near Savannah reproduced with
permission of Corbis (© Bettmann).

The author would like to thank Fergus M.
Bordewich for his helpful contributions during
the writing of this book.

Page 11: From UNCHAINED MEMORIES
by Henry L. Gates Jr., Spencer Crew, and
Cynthia Goodman. Copyright (c) 2003 by
Home Box Office, a division of Time Warner
Entertainment Company, L.P. By permission
of Bulfinch. All rights reserved.

CONTENTS

Some words are shown in bold, **like this**. You can find out what they mean by looking in the glossary.

A BID FOR FREEDOM

Charles Gilbert was a slave in the city of Richmond, Virginia in the United States. His master, Benjamin Davis, was keen to sell him for a good price. As Benjamin was plotting to sell Charles, the young man was planning his escape. He made contact with a ship's captain, who promised to transport him to freedom if he could make his way to Old Point Comfort, which was 260 kilometres (160 miles) from Richmond.

Many of Charles's relatives lived in Old Point Comfort, so Charles knew his master would seek him there. He would have to lie low until the ship's departure. He found a gloomy spot under a hotel, where he hid for four weeks. Charles emerged only under the cover of darkness to gather food from the hotel's slop tub which contained the guests' waste food. One day, he was almost discovered by a boy. Charles barked like a dog to frighten away the child. The trick worked, but Charles knew it was time to move on.

After spending a night up a tree, his next hiding place was at the **washhouse** of his slave friend Isabella. Unable to stay with her openly, he lifted the floorboards and hid underneath. Yet slave hunters came searching for

▼ This painting, based on *The Underground Railroad* by Charles T. Webber (1825–1911), shows **abolitionists** Levi and Catherine Coffin, and Hannah Haydock, helping a group of fugitive slaves.

HISTORY DETECTIVES: SOURCES

A **primary source** is a source created at the time being studied and provides evidence of life at the time. Primary sources include reports, letters, diaries, photographs, and paintings. We know about Charles Gilbert from a primary source. When he reached Philadelphia, he told his story to William Still (see page 8) who published it. Other primary sources about slave escapes include books written by **fugitives** and interviews carried out with former slaves. You can find these in the library or on the internet. These are useful primary sources. Yet not all materials produced at the time are useful.

Secondary sources interpret primary sources. They include history books and encyclopedias. They often include images or quotes from primary sources.

him, so he fled back to the hotel and then to the woods, where he again had to imitate a dog to avoid being detected. Meanwhile, Charles's mother had heard her son was attempting escape; she saved up some money, and a passage was booked for him on a steamer going to Philadelphia. Charles was overjoyed. He opted to spend his last night at Isabella's wash-house.

A NARROW ESCAPE

Shortly after Charles's arrival, three officers came looking for him. He had not yet hidden but was upstairs in a bedroom. To his great alarm, he heard an officer climbing up the stairs. Would they discover him, just hours before his departure?

Resourceful as ever, Charles quickly donned a dress and large bonnet that he found in the bedroom. Downstairs he went, the bonnet neatly covering his face. An officer asked his name and to whom he belonged. Charles, inventing some names, answered in a sweet, high voice. And he left the house, to board the steamer for Philadelphia and freedom.

WHY DID PEOPLE ESCAPE SLAVERY?

Why did Charles Gilbert and other slaves try to escape? To answer that question, we need to investigate slavery in the United States. Primary sources can help us. For example, we can read the laws of the time, which explain how slaves were legal property, like houses or animals. You can find evidence in newspapers from the time that indicate the effects of the laws and people's attitudes towards slavery.

The laws gave slaves no legal rights. They could not vote, own property, or marry. Slaves could not go anywhere without their master's permission. Slave owners could sell their slaves to another person, so families were often separated. Sometimes a father or mother was sold, or children were sold away from their parents.

HISTORY DETECTIVES: LAWS

Laws show us the policies of the government at the time. Virginia's slave codes of 1705 stated that all non-white people could be enslaved and punished by masters as they wished:

> All servants imported and brought into the Country ... who were not Christians in their native Country ... shall be accounted and be slaves. All Negro, mulatto [mixed race] and Indian slaves within this dominion [territory] ... shall be held to be real estate [property]. If any slave resist[s] his master ... and shall happen to be killed in such correction ... the master shall be free of all punishment ... as if such accident never happened.

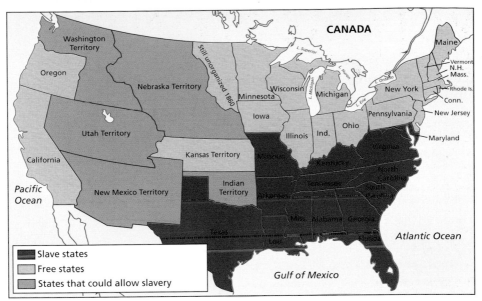

Washington
Territory

Oregon

Nebraska Territory

Still unorganized 1860

CANADA

L. Superior

L. Huron

L. Michigan

L. Ontario

L. Erie

Maine

Vermont
N.H.
Mass.

Wisconsin
Minnesota
Michigan

New York

Rhode Is.
Conn.

Iowa

Pennsylvania

New Jersey

Ohio

Utah Territory

California

Kansas Territory

Illinois

Ind.

Missouri

Virginia

Maryland

Pacific
Ocean

New Mexico Territory

Indian
Territory

Kentucky

North
Carolina

Tennessee

Arkansas

South
Carolina

Miss. Alabama Georgia

Texas

La.

Florida

Atlantic Ocean

Gulf of Mexico

- Slave states
- Free states
- States that could allow slavery

▲ This map shows the division of the United States into free and slave states in 1860.

HARSH CONDITIONS

The Northern states had abolished slavery by the early 19th century, but the Southern states depended on it. Their economy was based on farming **plantations**. Plantation owners used slave labour to work the land.

Slaves commonly endured harsh conditions. They usually worked from sunrise to sunset, with brief rests to eat. Children as young as six had to work. Slaves could not choose their job, and they received no pay. Sometimes their owners hired them out to do skilled jobs, but usually took all their wages. Slave owners provided food and clothing, which was often insufficient. However, farm slaves were usually allowed to grow some crops for themselves and raise chickens, so they could earn a little money – which some saved up to fund their escape.

BRUTAL PUNISHMENT

Slave owners punished their slaves if they believed they had not worked hard enough or had made a mistake. They might whip and beat them until they dripped with blood. Sometimes they **branded** them or cut off an ear. A slave thought to have committed a serious crime was killed.

WHAT LED PEOPLE TO ESCAPE?

We know that life was tough for slaves, but what made them decide to risk escaping? Slaves were rarely allowed to read and write, so first-person primary sources explaining their feelings are limited; around 120 former slaves produced a book about their experiences.

Only a tiny proportion of slaves wrote books, so **oral history** accounts are extremely important. William Still was a free African American who helped escaping slaves. When they stayed at his house in Philadelphia to rest on the way to freedom, he wrote down their stories. In 1872, after slavery ended in the United States, he published them in a huge book, along with letters and newspaper articles. William Still documents a variety of reasons why slaves ran away.

HARRIET JACOBS

Slave women were frequently forced to have a sexual relationship with their master. When Harriet Jacobs's master told her he would build her a house 6 kilometres (4 miles) away from her town in a quiet place so that he could spend time with her there, she knew he would press her into such a relationship. She told her remarkable story in a book, *Incidents in the Life of a Slave Girl*, which was published in 1861. Harriet explained how she decided to escape:

When my master said he was going to build a house for me ... I was in hopes something would happen to frustrate his scheme; but I soon heard that the house was actually begun. I vowed before my Maker [God] that I would never enter it: I had rather toil on the plantation from dawn till dark; I had rather live and die in jail, than drag on, from day to day, through such a living death ... What could I do? I thought and thought, till I became desperate, and made a plunge into the abyss.

You can read more of Harriet's story at: www.pagebypagebooks. com/Harriet_Jacobs/Incidents_in_the_Life_of_a_Slave_Girl/A_ Perilous_Passage_In_The_Slave_Girls_Life_p1.html

INCIDENTS

IN THE

LIFE OF A SLAVE GIRL.

WRITTEN BY HERSELF.

———————•———————

"Northerners know nothing at all about Slavery. They think it is perpetual bondage only. They have no conception of the depth of *degradation* involved in that word, SLAVERY; if they had, they would never cease their efforts until so horrible a system was overthrown."
A WOMAN OF NORTH CAROLINA.

"Rise up, ye women that are at ease! Hear my voice, ye careless daughters! Give ear unto my speech."
ISAIAH xxxii. 9.

———————

EDITED BY L. MARIA CHILD.

———————

BOSTON:
PUBLISHED FOR THE AUTHOR.
1861.

This is the title page from Harriet Jacobs's autobiography, which she published under the pseudonym (false name) Linda Brent. ▶

IN FEAR OF THEIR LIVES

Many fled because they could no longer tolerate their conditions and felt nothing could be worse than slavery. Theophilus Collins from Delaware escaped in 1858. After refusing to be whipped in punishment for attending a church service (masters often forbade slaves to attend church), Theophilus's master viciously attacked him. Theophilus told William Still: "He … told me if I ventured to the door he would stab me … before I reached it he stabbed me, drawing the knife (a common pocket knife) as hard as he could rip across my stomach." After a huge struggle, Theophilus got away, holding his stomach together. He was treated by doctors and, amazingly, he survived.

STORIES FROM *SLAVE NARRATIVES*

William Still's book containing fugitives' stories was the most significant primary-source account of the time. Decades later, in the 1930s, a major oral history project took place, financed by the **Works Progress Administration (WPA)**. Researchers talked to more than 2,300 former slaves, then over 80 years old, and in 1941 published their tales in *Slave Narratives*.

ABOUT TO BE SOLD

Some slaves fled because they were about to be sold. Alfred S. T. Hornton from Virginia was well-treated, but fled when he saw a slave trader approaching. He ran to his master, with the trader firing his revolver at him. Alfred pleaded with his master to explain why he had sold him, but to no avail. So Alfred fled as fast as he could, with nothing but the clothes on his back.

▼ An 1854 engraving of Louisville, Kentucky, which is on the Ohio River, a border between the Southern and Northern states. There were three crossing points from Louisville used by runaway slaves.

ROWING TO FREEDOM

WPA researcher Martin Richardson uncovered the fascinating story of Arnold Gragston, a 97-year-old former slave. It had never occurred to Arnold to flee until other slaves asked him to row them across the Ohio River:

> I didn't have no idea of ever gettin' mixed up in any sort of business like that until one special night ... But one night I had gone on another plantation courtin' [to meet girls], and [an] old woman ... told me she had a real pretty girl there who wanted to go across the river and would I take her?

> ... I don't know how I ever rowed the boat across the river[,] the current was strong and I was trembling.

> ... That was my first trip; it took me a long time to get over my scared feelin', but I finally did, and I soon found myself goin' back across the river, with two and three people, and sometimes a whole boatload.

> ... Finally, I saw that I could never do any more good in Mason County, so I decided to take my freedom, too. I had a wife by this time, and one night we quietly slipped across.

HISTORY DETECTIVES: SLAVE NARRATIVES

This primary source is extremely valuable to historians because it provides the stories of thousands of former slaves. Yet the information may not be completely accurate. Firstly, the storytellers were all over 80 and were remembering events of decades ago. They might have forgotten important events or muddled up facts. Secondly, many of the interviewers were white. The former slaves may not have felt entirely comfortable talking openly with white interviewers and might not have mentioned some of their harshest experiences.

WHAT WAS THE UNDERGROUND RAILROAD?

The Underground **Railroad** did not operate under the ground, and it was not a railroad or railway! It was a secret network of people who aided fugitives to flee into the free states. It provided them with safe places to stay on their journey to free states in the United States or elsewhere. The Underground Railroad probably began in the 1790s, in Philadelphia, and was most active from the 1830s to the 1860s. Some people assisted occasionally, while others were involved for decades, and the routes changed frequently. The Underground Railroad did not exist everywhere; many slaves had little, if any, help escaping.

THE FUGITIVE SLAVE ACT, 1850

Slave owners in the South were angry about losing their human property in the North. The Fugitive Slave Act was passed to make it easier for them to get their property back from another state. Citizens were expected to help. The law stated that those caught assisting fugitives could be fined US $1,000 (about £18,000 today) and be sent to prison for six months. This section explains that slave owners were permitted to seize back their slaves:

> when a person held to service or labor in any State or Territory of the United States ... shall ... escape into another State or Territory of the United States, the person ... to whom such service or labor may be due ... may pursue and reclaim such fugitive person, either by procuring [getting] a **warrant** from some one of the courts ... or by seizing and arresting such fugitive.

A SECRET ORGANIZATION

Underground Railroad operators in the North usually had to work secretly, especially after 1850 when the Fugitive Slave Act brought in tough new rules against assisting slaves to escape. Fugitives and their helpers were in greater danger than before. However, in some strongly abolitionist areas, such as parts of Ohio and Michigan, the Railroad could operate quite openly.

WORKING UNDERGROUND

People working for the Underground Railroad sometimes communicated through coded messages. Apart from other anti-slavery activists in their own community, they tended to know only a few other people involved at the next underground station. That way, if caught, they had very little information to pass on. If a route became unsafe because fugitives had been discovered, it would rapidly be changed.

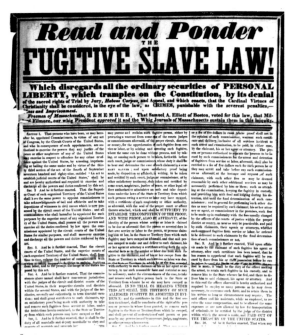

▲ This newspaper editorial from 1850 was opposed to the Fugitive Slave Law. An editorial gives the view of the editor and is a useful primary source for opinions at the time.

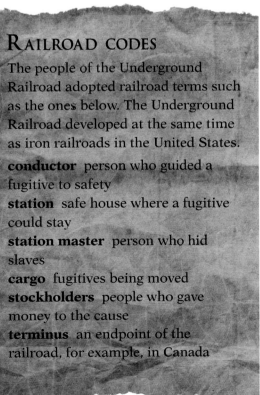

RAILROAD CODES

The people of the Underground Railroad adopted railroad terms such as the ones below. The Underground Railroad developed at the same time as iron railroads in the United States.

conductor person who guided a fugitive to safety

station safe house where a fugitive could stay

station master person who hid slaves

cargo fugitives being moved

stockholders people who gave money to the cause

terminus an endpoint of the railroad, for example, in Canada

RARE RECORDS

After the Fugitive Slave Act of 1850, conductors usually destroyed records of fugitives so that nobody would be able to trace them. Few records still exist. A rare example is the diary of David Putnam, a member of the Underground Railroad in Point Harmar, in Ohio. It notes the arrival and departure of fugitives:

> Aug. 13/[18]43
> Sunday Morn. 2 o'clock arrive
> Sunday Eve. 8 ½ o'clock dep.
> For B.

HISTORY DETECTIVES: UNDERGROUND RAILROAD CODE

Can you work out what these coded messages mean? See page 63 for the answers.

1. Joe, I have two black steers and a brown heifer at my house.

2. There is a chance to purchase a horse that will suit your purpose. He is a mahogany bay, young, well broken, large, and is just the thing for a minister. You can see him on Tuesday afternoon. Price $100.

▲ This was the New York City home of Isaac T. Hopper, a Quaker and an important member of the Underground Railroad.

VIEWS OF THE UNDERGROUND RAILROAD

Our understanding of the Underground Railroad has changed over time, and new information is still being revealed today. For example, by the 20th century, many people believed it was abolitionist white people alone who ran the Underground Railroad. These abolitionists mainly came from religious groups, such as the **Quakers**, that believed slavery was wrong. This viewpoint of the Underground Railroad arose because white abolitionists were in the best position to write about its activities.

▲ A painting of Jermain Loguen by 20th-century artist Jerry Pinkney, one of 12 portraits Pinkney painted to remember anti-slavery activists.

During the 20th century, interest in the Underground Railroad grew as part of the expansion of research into black history. It developed further in the 1990s through a federal programme to identify and preserve sites linked to the Railroad. Many local Underground Railroad research groups emerged, mostly in the North. Historians and local researchers discovered newspaper articles and letters, out-of-print **memoirs**, diaries, and other documents in libraries and archives. The recently developed internet allowed them to share the information. Significantly, researchers uncovered material about the large number of African Americans, both free and enslaved, who were heavily involved in the network. The roles of important black leaders, such as David Ruggles, Jermain Loguen, and George DeBaptiste, became better known.

THE QUAKERS

The Quakers were a minority Christian group who believed in plain living, human rights, and helping their community. Opposed to slavery for religious reasons, they initially formed the backbone of the white abolitionist movement. For them, anti-slavery work was a religious action. Even though only a minority of Quakers were involved in the Underground Railroad, other Quakers never betrayed their activities. This meant it was easy for fugitives to "disappear" in their communities.

DAVID RUGGLES, FUGITIVE PROTECTOR

David Ruggles was a **free black** man who organized the Underground Railroad in New York City in the 1830s, in collaboration with white and black allies. He formed a **Vigilance Committee**, an organization of African Americans to protect fugitives from capture by slave hunters and return to slavery in the South. He also called for greater equality for black people in the North. David died young, and his story was forgotten for many years.

In the early 21st century, David Ruggles finally received the recognition he deserved. In 2009, the David Ruggles Center opened in Florence, Massachusetts, to provide information about Ruggles and the Underground Railroad. The following year, historian Graham Russell Gao Hodges published the first-ever biography of Ruggles.

David Ruggles is just one of many. Historians realize that countless other black Americans participated in the Underground Railroad, and they continue to hunt for traces of their activities.

▼ This 1851 cartoon is based on the myth that only white abolitionists helped black slaves.

HISTORY DETECTIVES:
MYTHS ABOUT THE UNDERGROUND RAILROAD

Our job as historians is to sift through materials and sort fact from fiction. The Underground Railroad was a largely secret organization, so it is sometimes hard to discover the truth. There are some things we may never know for certain.

The name:
No one knows exactly where the term *Underground Railroad* came from. Various theories exist. According to one legend, in 1831 a fugitive from Kentucky called Tice Davids swam across the Ohio River. His master and other slave catchers were hot on his tail. But Tice Davids got away – perhaps anti-slavery activists assisted him. The slave owner apparently commented: "He must have gone off on an underground road." However, it is likely that this story is false.

The songs:
It is commonly believed that slaves used songs to inform others about the Underground Railroad routes or code words. One example is the song "Follow the Drinking Gourd", which supposedly included escape instructions and a map. The drinking gourd refers to the hollow gourds that rural Americans used as a water dipper. In the song, it is a code name for the Big Dipper – the group of stars that point to the North Star, which helped fugitives to navigate northwards. Historians are still debating the role of songs in the Underground Railroad, but as yet, there is no historical evidence that there was a system for using songs.

The quilts:
It was claimed in the 1990s that people hung quilts from roofs and barns to show fugitives that the place was a station on the Underground Railroad. However, quilts are not mentioned in any 19th-century slave narratives or the 20th-century *Slave Narratives*. No one has ever found a quilt known to have been used during the Underground Railroad. So there is no primary-source evidence for the use of quilts.

WHO USED THE UNDERGROUND RAILROAD?

How do we know who travelled on the Underground Railroad? William Still's comprehensive 1872 book, *The Underground Railroad*, published just after the end of slavery, revealed evidence to the American people. As well as his interviews with the fugitives who sheltered at his home, it contains letters, newspaper articles, and legal documents.

TRAVELLERS OF ALL AGES

William Still's book shows that most travellers were fit and healthy men aged between 20 and 40. Their youth and strength gave them the best chance of enduring the journey. Yet these men who fled alone had to make the terrible choice between freedom and family. Still demonstrated that fugitives also included men, women, and children of all ages. Fugitives were black and mixed-race slaves – some were so pale-skinned that they could "pass" for white. Occasionally, a white companion accompanied a fugitive.

▲ Here you can see slaves, some of them children, picking cotton in the Southern states. Some children travelled the Underground Railroad alone.

A SAFE ARRIVAL

Thomas Garrett, an Underground Railroad station master based in Wilmington, Delaware, wrote to William Still to announce the safe arrival of Ann Maria Jackson:

Wilmington, 11th mo. [November], 21st, 1858.

Dear Friends–[James Miller] McKim and Still:—I write to inform you that on the 16th of this month, we passed on four able bodied men to Pennsylvania, and they were followed last night by a woman and her six [perhaps this should have said "seven"] children, from three to four years of age, up to sixteen years… we had some trouble in getting those last safe along, as they could not travel far on foot, and could not safely cross any of the bridges on the canal, either on foot or in carriage. A man left here two days since, with carriage, to meet them this side of the canal, but owing to spies they did not reach him till 10 o'clock last night; this morning he returned, having seen them about one or two o'clock this morning in a second carriage, on the border of Chester county, where I think they are all safe…

Yours, Thos. Garrett.

William Still described the flight of Ann Maria Jackson and seven of her nine children (two had already been sold) from Maryland in 1859. She was prompted to run away by the news that four more of her children were to be sold. Her husband was too scared to leave, so she took charge of the escape. As Still noted: "The fire of freedom obviously burned with no ordinary fervor in the breast of this slave mother, or she never would have ventured with the burden of seven children, to escape from the hell of Slavery."

Think About This

Fleeing with children

Consider the difficulties of escaping with babies and small children. Which needs could it be hard to meet on the journey, and what risks would the youngsters present to the group?

SLAVES IN THE NORTH

The Underground Railroad in the North did not only help fugitives who had already made their escape. Vigilance Committees protected the rights of free blacks and encouraged slaves to flee bondage (slavery). According to the law in many states, including Pennsylvania, if a slave owner brought his or her property to the North, the slave automatically became free. When Underground Railroad activists heard of slaves being brought to their town, they informed them of their rights.

William Still wrote to the *New York Tribune* on 30 July 1855 to explain how he and a colleague, Passmore Williamson, discovered that Jane Johnson and her two sons had been brought to Philadelphia. The men hurried to board the ship:

> *Mr. W. and myself ran on board of the boat, looked among the passengers on the first deck, but saw them not. "They are up on the second deck," an unknown voice uttered. In a second we were in their presence. We approached the anxious-looking slave-mother with her two boys on her left-hand; close on her right sat an ill-favored white man…*

▼ This engraving from William Still's book shows escaped slaves fighting back against slave catchers.

The first words to the mother were: "Are you traveling?" "Yes," was the prompt answer. "With whom?" She nodded her head toward the ill-favored man ... Fidgeting on his seat, he said something ... In reply I remarked: "Do they belong to you, Sir?" "Yes, they are in my charge," was his answer. Turning from him to the mother and her sons ... the following remarks were ... addressed by the individuals who rejoiced to meet them on free soil ... informing them of their rights:

> *"You are entitled to your freedom according to the laws of Pennsylvania, having been brought into the State by your owner."*

Jane Johnson opted to leave her master, and with the help of the Underground Railroad, travelled with her children to Canada.

HISTORY DETECTIVES:
LETTERS TO NEWSPAPERS

We know about Jane Johnson from a newspaper article published by William Still. As a history detective, ask yourself some questions when considering this primary source as evidence. For example:

- Who wrote the article and what difference might this make?

- Is the report one-sided or does he give other people's opinions?

- Who is the intended audience? How might this have influenced the way he wrote the article?

UNUSUAL TRAVELLERS

The majority of travellers on the Underground Railroad were fugitives who were easily identifiable as slaves by the colour of their skin. However, William Still recorded some incredible stories that showed that the division of races in America was literally just skin deep. Many slaves had mixed parentage. Some were so pale-skinned that they could 'pass' as white – you could not tell their black heritage from looking at them. These slaves could use their appearance to their advantage in their escape plans.

HISTORY DETECTIVES: USING CENSUS FIGURES

Few fugitives left a record of their movements; most could not write, and it would have been dangerous to reveal their plans. So it is difficult to find out where they came from. The Canadian **census** of 1861 is a useful primary source. It shows that 80 per cent of Southern-born black people living in Canada came from Virginia, Maryland, and Kentucky – states that bordered the North. Few were able to make the long journey from states further south.

A CLEVER PLOT

Still recorded the following clever plot. David, a light-skinned 27-year-old slave from Leesburg, Virginia, was owned by Joshua Pusey. David hatched a plan to bolt with a white female friend and her daughter. They would look like a white family:

> David had no taste for Slavery, indeed, felt that it would be impossible for him to adapt himself to a life of servitude [slavery] for the special benefit of others; he had, already ... been dealt with very wrongfully by Pusey, who had deprived him of many years of the best part of his life... So after thinking of various plans, he determined not to run off as a slave with his "budget on his back," [as a poor man] but to "travel as a coach-man," under the "protection of a white lady." In planning this pleasant scheme, David was not blind to the fact that neither himself nor the "white lady" ... possessed either horse or carriage.

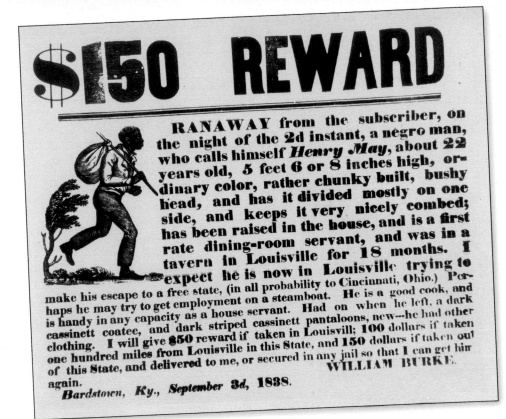

▲ A typical newspaper advertisement from a slave owner seeking help to find a fugitive slave and offering a generous reward.

But his master happened to have a vehicle that would answer for the occasion. David reasoned that as Joshua … had deprived him of his just dues for so many years, he had a right to borrow … one of Joshua's horses for the expedition.

Upon reaching Philadelphia, the group sought assistance from the Vigilance Committee. The Underground Railroad helped everyone who was trying to weaken the institution of slavery, whatever the colour of his or her skin.

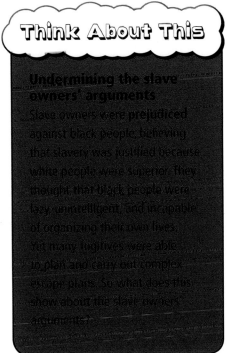

Think About This

Undermining the slave owners' arguments

Slave owners were prejudiced against black people, believing that slavery was justified because white people were superior. They thought that black people were lazy, unintelligent, and incapable of organizing their own lives. Yet many fugitives were able to plan and carry out complex escape plans. So what does this show about the slave owners' arguments?

HOW DID FUGITIVES ESCAPE?

Canadian dentist Dr Bryan Walls is descended from fugitive slaves. As a child, he listened to stories told by his Aunt Stella, the family storyteller. Born in the late 19th century, she heard fugitives' stories first-hand. Stella continued to tell stories until she died in 1986, aged 102.

Bryan was fascinated by Aunt Stella's tales of the Underground Railroad. She recounted that their ancestor John Freeman Walls was born in 1813 in Rockingham County, North Carolina. He made his bid for freedom in 1846. With the assistance of the Underground Railroad, John reached Maidstone in Ontario, Canada. As an adult, Bryan researched his fascinating family history and wrote a novel about it.

COURAGE FROM GOD

John Thompson, a fervent Christian, believed he gained the courage to flee slavery from God. Always under suspicion because he could write, there was a rumour that John had forged **passes** to allow slaves to escape. This was a serious offence. John did not know what to do. He was a few kilometres from home, planning to go back:

> ... when suddenly my steps were arrested, and a voice seemed to say, don't go any farther in that direction. I stopped, considered a moment, and concluded that it was mere fancy or conceit. So I started on again; but the same feelings returned with redoubled force.
>
> What can all this mean? I queried within myself; these sensations so strange and unusual; yet so strong and irresistable [sic]? It was God, warning me to avoid danger by not going home.

Read more from *The Life of John Thompson, a Fugitive Slave* at docsouth.unc.edu/neh/thompson/thompson.html

A LONG WALK

Like John Freeman Walls, many fugitives walked hundreds of kilometres to the North or all the way to Canada, often following rivers because the water hid their scent from slave hunters with dogs. If they were lucky, they found some help along the way from the Underground Railroad.

WHO IN HISTORY

FREDERICK DOUGLASS
About **1818–1895**
BORN: Tuckahoe, Maryland

ROLE: Leading abolitionist.
Born a slave, Douglass learnt to read and write, although this was illegal in Maryland. In 1833, he and three others tried to escape, but their plot was discovered. Five years later, Douglass succeeded in fleeing to New York City and then moving to New Bedford, Massachusetts. He changed his surname from Bailey to Douglass at this time to fool slave hunters. From 1841, he worked for the Massachusetts Anti-Slavery Society, speaking out about his experiences under slavery. Frederick wrote his autobiography in 1845. Fearing this would lead his former owner to track him down, he left for a two-year speaking tour of Britain to raise support for the abolitionist movement.

Did You Know?

During the American Civil War (1861–1865), Douglass met with President Abraham Lincoln. Many years later, he was made ambassador to Haiti.

A HELPING HAND

The Underground Railroad assisted many fugitives on their journey. Conductors accompanied their charges to the next station – a safe house where they would receive food, a change of clothes, and some money. There, the former slaves were told how to reach the following station. If they were to travel alone, a **runner** sometimes hurried to inform the station masters of the expected arrivals and provide a description. In this way, fugitives crossed the country to the Northern states or Canada.

Conductors usually led just one or two people or a small group. Years after the event, station master Levi Coffin (see page 33) described how his wife Catherine had greeted the arrival of an unusually large group of 17 fugitives at their home in Newport, Rhode Island:

> "What have you got there?" Catherine asked. "All Kentucky," one of the men replied. "Well, bring all Kentucky in," she answered.

With assistance from conductors, some fugitives travelled on horseback or by wagon, boat, or even train. When travelling by train, fugitives sometimes wore a disguise and carried false identity papers. William Still described how two young women got on the train to Philadelphia wearing black mourning clothes with heavy veils. When their master came into the carriage searching for his property, he failed to recognize them.

▼ Levi and Catherine Coffin. Catherine established a sewing circle to make good-quality clothes for fugitives, and was particularly caring towards fugitive women.

GEORGE DEBAPTISTE
1815–1875

BORN: Fredericksburg, Virginia

ROLE: A leader of the Underground Railroad.

George DeBaptiste came from a free black family. In 1837, he set up a barber's shop in Madison, Indiana. DeBaptiste and his friends assisted fugitives fleeing from Kentucky, just south of Indiana, across the Ohio River. He estimated that he himself helped 108 people, and on occasion, he even went to Kentucky to organize their escape. DeBaptiste worked for William Henry Harrison as his valet (personal servant) during Harrison's presidential campaign and as a **steward** in the White House. He returned to Madison after Harrison's death in 1841. Anti-black riots in 1845–1846 forced him to flee to Detroit, Michigan, where he continued his Underground Railroad activities.

Did You Know?

DeBaptiste sometimes walked 30 kilometres (20 miles) a night to conduct fugitives to a safe house, returning home to go to work the next day.

HISTORY DETECTIVES:
AFRICAN AMERICAN UNDERGROUND WORK

Historian Fergus M. Bordewich explains that in many communities close to the Ohio River, African Americans were responsible for most Underground Railroad activity. One example is the river port of Madison, Indiana, where George DeBaptiste operated. However, there are few primary sources from the people themselves because they did not leave diaries. White abolitionists sometimes mention them in their accounts, and their names occasionally appear in newspaper reports. More historical detective work is required in this area.

PACKED UP IN A BOX

In their desperation to reach freedom, some fugitives adopted hazardous plans. Some hid in woods or swamps for months, stowed away on ships, or even had themselves transported as cargo.

In 1851, people in England were astonished to read the autobiography of Henry "Box" Brown, published during the author's stay there. Here he describes entering a box in which he was shipped to Philadelphia:

> *The box which I had procured was three feet one inch wide, two feet six inches high, and two feet wide: and on the morning of the 29th day of March, 1849, I went into the box – having previously bored three gimlet holes opposite my face, for air, and provided myself with a bladder of water, both for the purpose of quenching my thirst and for wetting my face, should I feel getting faint... Being thus equipped for the battle of liberty, my friends nailed down the lid and had me conveyed to the Express Office, which was about a mile distant from the place where I was packed. I had no sooner arrived at the office than I was turned heels up, while some person nailed something on the end of the box. I was then put upon a waggon and driven off to the depôt with my head down, and I had no sooner arrived at the depôt, than the man who drove the waggon tumbled me roughly into the baggage car, where, however, I happened to fall on my right side.*

▼ A 19th-century illustration of the moment when Henry "Box" Brown was released from his box. In reality, he probably would have looked less neat and tidy!

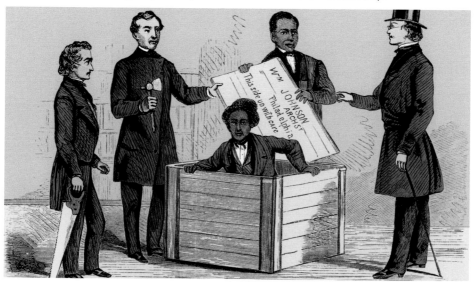

After a 27-hour journey, Henry "Box" Brown arrived. William Still and three abolitionists opened the box and Brown emerged, saying "How do you do, Gentlemen?"

But we will never know how many escapes failed. Some fugitives were killed in the attempt, while others were returned to slavery; in most cases, their story died with them.

Think About This

Fugitives and refugees
Compare primary-source Underground Railroad accounts with first-hand accounts of **refugees** today. Who helps refugees now? Which desperate measures do they adopt to reach freedom? Consider the similarities and differences.

WHO IN HISTORY

HENRY "BOX" BROWN
1815/6–AFTER 26 FEBRUARY 1889
BORN: Louisa County, Virginia

ROLE: Abolitionist and performer.
Born into slavery, Henry worked in a tobacco factory in Richmond. In 1848, his pregnant wife Nancy and their three children were sold to a plantation owner in North Carolina. After months of grief, Henry decided to ship himself to Philadelphia in a wooden crate. A free black dentist and a white shoemaker agreed to help. As a free man, Henry lectured and performed a show about slavery. After the Fugitive Slave Act of 1850, he was nearly kidnapped, so he fled to England, where he continued his anti-slavery work. In 1875, Henry returned to the United States with his English wife and daughter. Read the *Narrative of the Life of Henry Box Brown* at docsouth.unc.edu/neh/brownbox/brownbox.html.

Did You Know?

No one knows when or where Henry "Box" Brown died. Perhaps a historian will find out one day.

WHERE DID FUGITIVES GO?

The main Underground Railroad routes went to the Northern US states and Canada. Once fugitives had escaped the slave states, there was a variety of Underground Railroad routes northwards, for example through Ohio, Indiana, Illinois, Philadelphia, New York State, and Massachusetts.

Large numbers of fugitives crossed the Ohio River. Along the river, there were a dozen popular crossing points, and stations were found on both sides – for example, in Maysville, Kentucky and in Madison, Indiana.

▼ This map shows the variety of routes taken by fugitive slaves within the United States and also to Canada, the Caribbean, and South America.

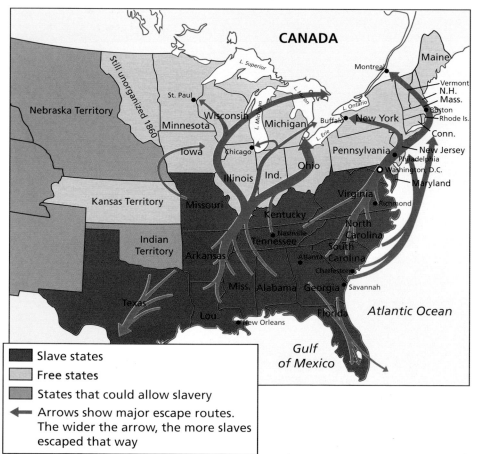

Slave states
Free states
States that could allow slavery
◀── **Arrows show major escape routes. The wider the arrow, the more slaves escaped that way**

A DRAMATIC DEPARTURE

As a boy, Eugene Settles from Ripley, Ohio, heard the heroic tale of his grandfather Joseph Settles, who was born into slavery:

Joseph Settles was my grandfather, and he came from Maysville, where he was raised... My grandfather ran off to keep from being sold and he brought 12 people with him – he made two trips on two different nights. He had made friends with a lot of people in Maysville, and one of his friends was a white man, of course, who had a boat ... and he let him use that boat ... he made two trips. The first night they landed out here ... and he let them out. And he went back and hld the boat in the willows or some place... The second night ... they had his young daughter with a young baby with her. There were patarollers, people who were trying to catch the runaway slaves. They came to a big, high fence, and these people were trying to catch them – they could hear them right behind. The older people climbed over the fence. The young baby was crying. [My grandfather's] brother-in-law pitched him over the fence. They [the patarollers] were that close behind them that second night.

HISTORY DETECTIVES:
ARE FAMILY STORIES RELIABLE EVIDENCE?

When stories are passed down from generation to generation, the story may change because of the viewpoint and circumstances of the teller. In the Settles' case, early retellings took place under slavery. Storytellers would not have revealed the names of the fugitives or exactly where they went. In general, storytellers tend to add details to make the tale more exciting. The next teller will include these new parts as fact, so the story gradually changes over time. Nevertheless, the core of the tale remains. It can be particularly useful to a historian if it confirms historical evidence found elsewhere. Researchers ideally like to have at least two different sources of a story as evidence.

FIRST STOP OHIO

One significant conductor on the northern bank of the Ohio River was John Parker. Yet until recently, little was known about him. John, a successful African American businessman, led a dual life. During the day, he ran an iron **foundry**, and at night, he risked his life by secretly entering the slave state of Kentucky to bring fugitives over the Ohio River in a boat. He then quietly delivered them to safe houses such as John Rankin's (see below). In the 1880s, John Parker recounted his experiences to a journalist, Frank M. Gregg, but they did not become widely known. In 1996, the interviews were edited and published as a book. His house has now been restored and is open to the public. John Parker now has his rightful place in history.

Far more is known about the **Presbyterian** minister John Rankin, a white conductor whose sons wrote about his work. He and his family lived in a house on a hill in Ripley, Ohio, overlooking the Ohio River. When it was safe for runaways over the border in Kentucky to cross, John signalled to them with a lantern. Around 2,000 fugitives escaped through Ripley, and most stayed with the Rankins.

◀ Around the United States today, people are working to preserve the memory of the Underground Railroad by maintaining well-known stations, such as Rankin House (on top of the hill) as museums.

WHO IN HISTORY

LEVI COFFIN
1798–1877
BORN: New Garden (now Greensboro), North Carolina

ROLE: Abolitionist, nicknamed "President of the Underground Railroad".
Although white and born in the South, Coffin was a Quaker who strongly opposed slavery. He moved to Newport (now Fountain City), Indiana, in 1826, which was on the route many fugitives took from the South to Canada. His home became an Underground Railroad station. Coffin was a merchant and used much of his money to help more than 3,000 fugitives. He moved to Cincinnati in 1847, where he continued to work with the Underground Railroad until the Civil War. His autobiography, *Reminiscences of Levi Coffin*, published in 1876, provided useful information about the anti-slavery movement.

Did You Know?

A slave called Sol worked tirelessly with Coffin and his family on the New Garden Underground Railroad. Sadly, Coffin recorded few details of Sol's important role.

WHY DID FUGITIVES HIDE?

Although slavery was illegal in Ohio, not everyone was in favour of ending it, so there was conflict between people who were pro- and anti-slavery. (This was true elsewhere in the North.) It was important for fugitives to stay in safe houses. Sometimes, they sheltered in attics, basements, under floorboards, or even in cupboards. But often they simply arrived late at night, slept in a spare bedroom, and departed at dawn for the next station. Few buildings provide visible evidence of the Underground Railroad because most safe houses were just ordinary homes.

UNEARTHING UNDERGROUND RAILROAD HISTORY

Many secrets of Underground Railroad locations are hidden in buildings or even under the ground. Local historians and archaeologists research known routes to reveal them.

THE STEPHEN AND HARRIET MYERS RESIDENCE

In the late 1990s, amateur local historians Paul and Mary Liz Stewart sought out new evidence that Albany in New York State was on the Underground Railroad route. The name of freed slave Stephen Myers came up repeatedly in their research. Other researchers told the Stewarts about an 1856 Vigilance Committee flier announcing a meeting at the Underground Railroad headquarters – the Myers' home. This was gold dust!

Yet there was still work to do. The address on the flier was 198 Lumber Street, which is now Livingstone Avenue. The houses had been renumbered a few times, so the Stewarts checked through old maps and house **deeds** to find out which house it was. Eventually, they worked out that 194 Livingstone Avenue was the one.

▼ Stephen and Harriet Myers' house, as it stands today.

HISTORY DETECTIVES:
WHAT CAN ARCHAEOLOGY TELL US?

Archaeology is the scientific study of the material remains of past human life and activities. Archaeologists look for objects made by human beings, such as tools and household goods, as well as the remains of buildings and other evidence of human activity. They describe and analyse the objects they find. Then they check the written sources from the time to see how the evidence from documents and from objects fits together. This leads to a greater understanding of the past. So archaeology is a vital part of historical research.

Excited by this discovery, in 2004, the Underground Railroad History Project, founded by Paul and Mary Liz, bought the property. Volunteers began work to restore the house to how it would have looked in the 1850s and turn it into an Underground Railroad museum. Find out more at metroland.net/back_issues/vol_27_no23/feature_2.html.

DIGGING UP RAMPTOWN

Another mystery Underground Railroad location was Ramptown, Michigan. At the start of the 21st century, local historian Sondra Mose-Ursery had heard rumours of a community of fugitive slaves there. But she said, "You'd ask people about Ramptown, and no one had heard about it." Since the inhabitants were fugitives, the settlement did not appear in official documents or on maps. People with first-hand knowledge of Ramptown had died long ago. There were many such black settlements in the North, which tended to be ignored by white communities.

Archaeology Professor Michael Nassaney of Western Michigan University aimed to find out. In 2002, his team searched in fields that were being ploughed in Penn and Calvin townships near Vandalia. They were delighted to find evidence of domestic households, including nails, horseshoes, glass, bricks, and pieces of pottery. In total, they found 1,143 **artefacts**, which proved that there must have been a settlement there. The team also investigated written and oral history accounts from the period, which backed up their discoveries. Ramptown was on the map again.

FLEEING TO CANADA

After the passage of the Fugitive Slave Act, slave owners could more easily seize fugitives back from the Northern states. Therefore, after reaching the North, many fugitives continued to Canada. In Canada, although there was prejudice against black people, they were legally equal. They could own property, vote, and be paid for their work. Families could stay together, and children could attend school. This was not always true in the North.

William Still recorded the experiences of a group of six fugitives who took advantage of the Christmas holiday in 1855 to flee Loudoun County, Virginia, and set out for Canada using their master's horses and carriage. On the way, a group of white men confronted them. But the fugitives had weapons and were prepared to use them, so the white group retreated. Two of the fugitives became separated from the group, however, and were apparently captured. The others reached Canada.

> ... one hundred miles from home ... they were attacked by "six white men, and a boy," who ... felt it to be their duty ... to demand of them an account of themselves...

> The spokesman amongst the fugitives ... told their assailants plainly, that "no gentleman would interfere with persons riding along civilly"... These "gentlemen," however, were not willing to accept this account of the travelers...

> At this juncture, the fugitives verily believing that the time had arrived for the practical use of their pistols and dirks [daggers], pulled them out of their concealment ... and declared they would not be "taken!"

BREAKING DOWN BARRIERS IN CANADA

After 1850, when the number of fugitives in Canada rose dramatically, the Colonial Church and School Society set up schools in Canada West (now western Ontario) for the children of fugitives. Other children could attend too, and the schools were successful. One school mistress commented that this success proved the "feasibility of educating together white and colored children". This was a radical view at the time.

WHO IN HISTORY

JOSIAH HENSON
1789–1883
BORN: Charles County, Maryland

ROLE: Methodist **preacher** and founder of a fugitive settlement. Born into slavery, Josiah Henson was trusted by his master and oversaw other slaves. In 1828, he toured as a preacher and earned enough money to buy his freedom, but his master betrayed and sold him. Henson fled with his wife and four children, reaching Canada in 1830. There, he worked as a farm labourer for a few years. In 1840, Henson and white supporters bought land to found Dawn, a settlement where former slaves could work the land. He also established an institute to educate the settlers and teach them useful trades. Henson published his autobiography in 1849. You can find it at docsouth.unc.edu/neh/henson49/henson49.html.

Did You Know?

Harriet Beecher Stowe used Josiah Henson's experiences as one of several sources to write the character of Uncle Tom in her 1852 novel *Uncle Tom's Cabin*.

FLEEING SOUTH: THE BLACK SEMINOLES

Not all fugitives escaped on the Underground Railroad. Before 1819, when Florida became part of the United States, some fugitives found protection with the Seminole American Indian peoples there. The fugitives joined the Seminoles and adopted their customs.

In June 2012, the US National Park Service sponsored a unique national conference for the reunion of Black Seminoles, the descendants of fugitives who had sought protection with the Seminoles. The conference reunited people whose ancestors had been scattered around the United States, Mexico, and the Bahamas. They met to expand their knowledge of this little-known aspect of fugitive history and to enjoy traditional music and dancing. The participants were living proof that a significant number of fugitives had fled south, survived, and thrived.

THE GREAT DISMAL SWAMP

Brave fugitives from Virginia and South Carolina fled to the Great Dismal Swamp, a forested, marshy area on the border of those two states. It provided an excellent hiding place for fugitives able to survive in the wild. Settlements of maroon (escaped slave) communities developed there.

THE WEST AND MEXICO

Other fugitives eventually found their way West to California, Alaska, and Hawaii. Former slave Felix Haywood from San Antonio, Texas, was interviewed by a WPA interviewer in the 1930s, aged 92. He explained how some fugitives fled to Mexico. Interestingly, Felix did not himself flee:

Sometimes someone would come 'long and try to get us to run up North and be free. We used to laugh at that. There wasn't no reason to run up North. All we had to do was walk, but walk South, and we'd be free as soon as we crossed the Rio Grande [river forming part of the border with Mexico]. In Mexico you could be free. They didn't care what color you was, black, white, yellow or blue. Hundreds of slaves did go to Mexico and got on all right.

In Disguise

Some fugitives travelled further to evade the clutches of their former masters. William and Ellen Craft made a plucky escape from Georgia. Able to pass as white, Ellen dressed as a plantation owner (see her in disguise below), with William as her servant. They managed to reach Boston. However, slave hunters tried to recapture them. The anti-slavery newspaper, the *Liberator*, reported on 1 November 1850:

> *Our city ... has been thrown into a state of intense excitement by the appearance of two prowling villains, named Hughes and Knight, from Macon, Georgia, for the purpose of seizing William and Ellen Craft, under the infernal Fugitive Slave Bill [Act], and carrying them back to the hell of Slavery. Since the day of '76 [1776: the year of the Declaration of Independence], there has not been such a popular demonstration on the side of human freedom in this region.*

WHAT WERE THE RISKS?

The hazards for fugitives were numerous. They ranged from getting cold and lost to being mauled by wild animals or captured by slave catchers. Underground Railroad helpers risked attack by opponents, arrest, and imprisonment. Yet many accepted the dangers in the cause of freedom.

FLEEING TO THE UNKNOWN

Many fugitives knew little about the area where they lived because they had never had the freedom to explore it. They had little or no money, or useful possessions such as warm clothes. Generally unable to read, they had to remember instructions from others. Some gave up after a short time. Easter Wells told a WPA interviewer about her mother:

> One day mammy burnt de bread... She knowed dat old Master would be mad and she'd be punished so she got some grub and her bonnet and she lit out. She hid in de woods and cane brakes [dense sugar-cane plants] for two weeks... Finally she come home and old Master give her a whipping... She told us dat she could'a slipped off to de North but she didn't want to leave us children. She was afraid Master would be mad and sell us.

UNCERTAINTY

Jim Pembroke lived in Maryland close to the border with the North and hoped to reach Pennsylvania: "But I knew not where its soil begins, or where that of Maryland ends... My only guide was the north star, by this I knew my general course northward, but at what point I should strike Penn, or when and where I should find a friend, I knew not."

It was common for fugitives to be concerned about reprisals against relatives. As he was about to flee, Francis Federic worried about his mother being harmed. He later told a WPA interviewer, "I could foresee how my master would stand over her with the lash to extort [force] from her my hiding-place."

Once fugitives had escaped, they were pursued. Slave owners patrolled the woods, and they kept dogs for tracking runaways. Recaptured fugitives faced severe punishment – usually a whipping or beating in front of other slaves, sometimes to within an inch of their lives.

▼ Slavery also existed in the Caribbean, among many other parts of the world. This 19th-century illustration shows a European overseer forcing one slave to whip another.

WEATHER HAZARDS

For travellers to the North, the winter could be the best time to escape because the Ohio River was frozen, and fugitives could walk across the ice. Also, slaves had some free time at Christmas, so their owners would not miss them for a few days. However, travelling in freezing conditions, often without adequate clothing, proved tough.

WILD ANIMALS

Fugitives sometimes had to hide away for months during their journey. William Jordon told William Still that it took him ten months to find the Underground Railroad. While he was waiting: "this brave-hearted young fugitive abode [lived] in the swamps – three months in a cave – surrounded with bears, wild cats, rattle-snakes and the like.

While in the swamps and cave, he was not troubled, however, about ferocious animals and venomous reptiles. He feared only man!"

STOWAWAYS RISKING SUFFOCATION

Some fugitives stowed away on cargo ships going north. Abraham Galloway and Richard Eden told William Still how they fled from North Carolina hiding in a vessel loaded with turpentine (strong-smelling paint cleaner). The slave owners of North Carolina were wise to this escape route, though. A law permitted them to smoke all ships going north. Usually, the fugitives could not breathe through the smoke, and revealed themselves. Cleverly, Abraham and Richard:

...devised a safe-guard against the smoke. This ... consisted in silk oil cloth shrouds, made large, with drawing strings, which, when pulled over their heads, might be drawn very tightly around their waists... A bladder of water and towels were provided, the latter to be wet and held to their nostrils should there be need.

In the end, it was the turpentine fumes that nearly killed them, but the pair survived their ordeal and made it to Canada.

SURVIVAL IN A CRAWLSPACE

Fugitive Harriet Jacobs (see pages 8–9) risked recapture and poor health for seven years, hiding in a tiny space above a porch of just 3 by 2 metres (9 by 7 feet), with a sloping ceiling. She later described her "Loophole of Retreat" in her autobiography:

> The air was stifling; the darkness total. A bed had been spread on the floor. I could sleep quite comfortably on one side; but the slope was so sudden that I could not turn on my other without hitting the roof. The rats and mice ran over my bed; but I was weary, and I slept such sleep as the wretched may, when a tempest has passed over them. Morning came. I knew it only by the noises I heard; for in my small den day and night were all the same. I suffered for air even more than for light.

Harriet Jacobs died in 1897. She is buried in Mount Auburn Cemetery in Cambridge, Massachusetts. ▶

THE DANGER OF SLAVE CATCHERS

Slave hunting was an organized industry. Slave catchers advertised their services in the newspapers, and slave owners paid them for returning their property. The slave catchers, often working with Northern lawyers and the authorities, travelled north to track down escaped slaves. Some Northern whites – and even a few free blacks – were prepared to betray fugitives to the slave catchers in return for a handsome fee.

Slave catchers intended to bring back their prey alive, but would attack fugitives if they ran away. Some fugitives managed to arm themselves in case they needed to fight back. William Still recorded the case of Wesley Harris, the leader of a party of fugitives who were betrayed and pursued by armed slave catchers: "Wesley bravely used his fire arms until almost fatally wounded by one of the pursuers, who with a heavily loaded gun discharged the contents with deadly aim in his left hand, which raked the flesh from the bone for a space of about six inches [15 centimetres]." He reached Philadelphia seriously injured. The Vigilance Committee provided medical attention; once he had recovered, Wesley went on to Canada.

▼ An illustration of the Christiana Riot (see opposite). Thirty-eight arrested men were charged with treason, because refusing to help slave catchers was considered to be a danger to the country.

HISTORY DETECTIVES:
VIEWS OF THE CHRISTIANA RIOT

Some Northern whites and African Americans defended fugitives from slave catchers. During the Christiana Riot of 1851, free African Americans fought a group of slave catchers from Maryland who were attempting to capture four fugitives. The slave owner was killed and two of his party were wounded. Following the battle, 37 African Americans and a white man were arrested and charged with **treason** under the Fugitive Slave Act, but none was convicted (found guilty).

From newspaper articles at the time, we know that some white people supported the fugitives, while others opposed them. Compare these extracts from an anti-abolitionist and an abolitionist newspaper discussing the hunt for the fugitives' defenders:

The unwarrantable [unreasonable] outrage committed last week, at Christiana, Lancaster county, is a foul stain upon the fair name and fame of our State. We are pleased to see that the officers of the Federal and State Governments are upon the tracks of those who were engaged in the riot, and that several arrests have been made.
Anti-abolitionist Philadelphia newspaper

Never did our heart bleed with deeper pity for the … persecuted colored people, than when we saw this troop let loose upon them, and witnessed the terror and distress which its approach excited in families, wholly innocent of the charges laid against them.
Abolitionist newspaper

THE PENALTIES FOR CONDUCTORS

Conductors risked stiff penalties for helping fugitives. Seaman Jonathan Walker revealed his astonishing story to abolitionist audiences in the North in the mid-1840s.

In 1844, Walker had hatched an extraordinary plan to rescue six fugitives by sailing in a small boat from Pensacola, Florida, to the British Bahamas – a treacherous journey of several weeks. The group were captured just one day before their arrival. Walker was arrested for slave stealing and branded on his hand with the letters "SS", standing for his crime. Branding was a punishment normally meted out to slaves, not to white people. Walker proudly declared to his listeners that the letters stood for "slave saviour". After a severe prison sentence, he was released; abolitionists paid his fines, and he embarked on lecture tours speaking against slavery.

JERMAIN LOGUEN, UNDERGROUND RAILROAD AGENT

Born into slavery, Jermain Loguen (see page 15) escaped to the North in 1834. In 1841, he became a preacher and established his home in Syracuse, New York as a station on the Underground Railroad. Despite the risks, Jermain was completely open about his activities. He placed adverts in the Syracuse newspapers asking for donations to assist fugitives. Jermain was not attacked because Syracuse was strongly abolitionist and he had influential white supporters.

You can read *The Rev. J. W. Loguen, as a Slave and as a Freeman. A Narrative of Real Life* at docsouth.unc.edu/neh/loguen/loguen.html.

VIOLENT ATTACK

Since the Underground Railroad was not entirely secret, conductors – African Americans in particular – were often attacked by pro-slavery opponents. In 1846, for example, Kentucky slave owners attempted to terrify Underground Railroad activists in Madison into giving up their work. A white mob attacked black people in their homes and beat them severely. Even white activists were attacked. In 1841, a group of Kentuckians launched an armed attack against John Rankin's home, which was ably resisted by his sons.

WHO IN HISTORY

HARRIET TUBMAN
About **1820–1913**

BORN: Dorchester County, Maryland

ROLE: Underground Railroad conductor and abolitionist. In 1849, hearing rumours that she was to be sold, Tubman left her family and fled north. She later returned to rescue her sister and her sister's two children. Risking recapture, Harriet made several more journeys South to lead fugitives to freedom, and became known as the "Moses" of her people (after Moses in the Bible who led the Jewish people out of Egypt). A strong leader, it is said she told her charges that if anyone tried to return to slavery, she would kill them – otherwise they might betray the group. She often travelled in disguise or pretended to be stupid so that no one suspected her of Underground Railroad activity.

Did You Know?

It is said that Harriet never lost a fugitive she was leading to freedom.

▼ In some areas, abolitionists could be open about their activities. This 1844 Chicago newspaper advertisement for the Liberty Line clearly refers to the Underground Railroad.

LIBERTY LINE.
NEW ARRANGEMENT---NIGHT AND DAY.

The improved and splendid Locomotives, Clarkson and Lundy, with their trains fitted up in the best style of accommodation for passengers, will run their regular trips during the present season, between the borders of the Patriarchal Dominion and Libertyville, Upper Canada. Gentlemen and Ladies, who may wish to improve their health or circumstances, by a northern tour, are respectfully invited to give us their patronage.

SEATS FREE, *irrespective of color.*

Necessary Clothing furnished gratuitously to such as have *"fallen among thieves."*

"Hide the outcasts—let the oppressed go free."—*Bible.*

☞For seats apply at any of the trap doors, or to the conductor of the train.

J. CROSS, *Proprietor.*

N. B. For the special benefit of Pro-Slavery Police Officers, an extra heavy wagon for Texas, will be furnished, whenever it may be necessary, in which they will be forwarded as dead freight, to the "Valley of Rascals," always at the risk of the owners.

☞Extra Overcoats provided for such of them as are afflicted with protracted *chilly-phobia.*

WHAT HAPPENED TO THE FUGITIVES?

Freedom in the North was not guaranteed. Fugitives might settle in a new city believing their former owner would not track them down. Suddenly, they would be seized by slave catchers and returned to bondage in the South. William Still catalogued some cases, for example: "Adam Gibson, a free colored man, residing in Philadelphia, was arrested, delivered into the hands of his alleged claimants, by commissioner Edward D. Ingraham, and hurried into Slavery."

RACISM IN THE NORTH

Although slavery was illegal in the North, there was **discrimination** against African Americans and **segregation** (forced separation from white people). Most states did not allow African Americans to vote. Some barred them from certain jobs or forbade them from inheriting property. Many states did not allow black people to access schools, public transport, or eating places. So African Americans and their white allies set up their own schools, churches, and other institutions.

▲ A portrait of William Still.

PROUD TO BE FREE

William Still also recorded countless letters from grateful fugitives who had achieved freedom, providing an excellent source of information about the lives of former slaves. They described their new situation in their letters. William Jones, who escaped slavery in 1859 by being transported as cargo in a box, wrote to Still from Albany, New York. He was clearly proud to be earning money for the first time: "… i am now in a store and getting sixteen dollars a month at the present… i have got a long without any trub le a tal [trouble at all]."

HISTORY DETECTIVES:
HOW RELIABLE WAS STILL'S BOOK?

William Still was the son of former slaves, a free African American, and an active member of the Underground Railroad. It was likely that fugitives were honest with him when relating their experiences. Nevertheless, when using primary-source evidence, we always need to be aware of the opinions of the author and the audience at the time.

William was writing for a broad American readership. He clearly desired to show African Americans in a positive light, as honest, intelligent human beings who should enjoy the same rights as white people. He frequently described the good looks, strength, and cleverness of the fugitives. This description from the Underground Railroad Records even gives the potential price of the fugitive, which seems ironic! "June 4, 1857. – Edward is a hardy and firm-looking young man of twenty-four years of age, chestnut color, medium size, and 'likely,' – would doubtless bring $1,400 in the market."

William was clearly biased in favour of ending slavery, but this does not mean that his book is unreliable. Historians believe that his contemporary accounts are some of the most accurate we have.

LIFE IN CANADA

We have valuable primary-source evidence of fugitives' new lives in Canada. In the early 1850s, white abolitionist Benjamin Drew travelled to Canada West (now Ontario), where around 30,000 black people lived, to interview fugitives. He compiled scores of personal histories and published them in a book in 1856, *Narratives of Fugitive Slaves in Canada*. Drew used fictitious names to protect his interviewees' identities and their relatives still living in the South. This is the only collection of first-hand interviews of fugitives in Canada (see docsouth.unc.edu/neh/drew/drew.html).

▼ These are the descendants of fugitive slaves and their white classmates in the class of 1909–1910 in North Buxten, Ontario, Canada. In some Canadian schools, black and white children were educated together (see page 36).

EDUCATION AND WORK

Benjamin Drew heard how the fugitives were attempting to establish themselves as free people. For those who had never learnt to read and write, obtaining an education was important. As William Grose explained to him:

> I have no education myself, but I don't intend to let my children come up as I did. I have but two, and instead of making servants out of them, I'll give them a good education, which I could not do in the southern portion of the United States.

Grose described how black people could work for themselves in Canada:

> ...the colored people are more sober and industrious than in the States: there they feel when they have money, that they cannot make what use they would like of it, they are so kept down, so looked down upon. Here they have something to do with their money, and put it to a good purpose.

FARMING THE FIELDS

Most former fugitives, with experience of working in the fields, became farmers. In Canada by the early 1840s, there were around 12,000 of them. There were even specially created settlements for black farmers, such as Dawn (see page 37). Yet although some fugitives became successful, many of the first generation to achieve freedom remained in poverty owing to a lack of resources and knowledge of how to run their own lives.

RESCUING RELATIVES

While appreciating their freedom, fugitives who had departed alone often hoped to be reunited with their families and some asked the Vigilance Committee to help their relatives to escape. William Still recorded many such letters. Joseph Ball sent a plea from Toronto, Canada, on 7 November 1857:

> Dear Mr. Still: – As I must again send you a letter fealing [sic] myself oblidge [sic] to you for all you have done and your kindness. Dear Sir my wife will be on to Philadelphia on the 8th 7th, and I would you to look out for her and get her an [sic] ticket and send her to me [in] Toronto. Her name are [sic] Mary Ball with five children. Please send her as soon as you can.

Alternatively, some former fugitives hired agents, either white or black, to go south and rescue relatives.

HARRIET TUBMAN: SOUTHERN MISSIONS

Some fugitives, such as Harriet Tubman, risked their new-found liberty to return South themselves to rescue relatives. Intrigued by Harriet Tubman, historian Milton C. Sernett, a specialist in the history of slavery and its abolition, published a book about her in 2007. This extraordinary woman had become so famous for her role as a conductor to freedom that for many Americans she was the only person they could name from the Underground Railroad.

Yet it is difficult to separate the truth about Harriet Tubman from the myth. Unable to read and write, she could not write a diary of her experiences. But she was an amazing storyteller who enjoyed telling young people of her adventures. These stories were passed on from person to person before they were written down. In 1886, Sarah Bradford published a biography of Harriet that included the claim that she rescued 300 people in 19 trips to the South.

▲ Harriet Tubman in old age. After working with the Underground Railroad, she served as a scout and spy for the Union forces during the Civil War (1861–1865).

When Sernett looked into it, he realized that there was very little primary-source evidence of Harriet's activities leading slaves to freedom. It had been too dangerous to publicize the details. Just a few scant primary sources exist, such as Thomas Garrett's letter to William Still.

CONDUCTOR TUBMAN

In 1854, station master Thomas Garrett from Delaware sent some fugitives to William Still with a letter:

We made arrangements last night, and sent away Harriet Tubman, with six men and one woman to Allen Agnew's to be forwarded across the country to the city. Harriet, and one of the man had worn their shoes off their feet, and I gave them two dollars to help fit them out, and directed a carriage to be hired at my expense, to take them out.

By looking at the available evidence, Sernett could account for only seven to nine of Harriet's trips South – the figure of 19 simply did not stand up to historical evidence. This does not diminish her courageous work, but it shows that legends can develop that are not based on solid evidence.

Since the early 1990s, historians have discovered the role of many other conductors, such as John Parker (see page 32), who also risked their lives to enter the South and free slaves. Continued research is likely to uncover more evidence of their courageous work.

HOW STORIES EVOLVE

Stories tend to change slightly every time they are retold. Try this out with a group of friends. One person whispers a very short story to the next person. He or she then recounts what they hear to the next person. Once everyone has had a chance to tell the story, ask the last person to say what they heard, and compare it to the original story. How much difference is there?

WHY WAS THE UNDERGROUND RAILROAD SIGNIFICANT?

The Underground Railroad helped to push the issue of slavery to the top of the agenda in US politics. The number of slaves escaping with its assistance put pressure on the system of slavery, and it became one of the key issues that led to the Civil War between the Northern and Southern states (1861–1865). The North won the war, and one significant result was the ending of slavery in 1865. In 1870, the 15th **Amendment** to the US **Constitution** permitted all men to vote. The Underground Railroad was no longer needed. As Levi Coffin commented, "Our work is done."

THE 15TH AMENDMENT

The 15th Amendment gave African American men – but not women – the right to vote. It stated that the "right of citizens of the United States to vote shall not be denied or abridged [reduced] by the United States or by any state on account of race, color, or previous condition of servitude [slavery]".

RESISTANCE TO SLAVERY

The Underground Railroad demonstrates the initiative of slaves, free blacks, and their helpers in resisting the institution of slavery. By discovering primary sources about many of these people, historians have realized that it was not just famous white abolitionists who participated – it was the enslaved themselves. It is important for African Americans today to know that their ancestors fought injustice.

The actions of fugitives showed the intelligence and resourcefulness of many African Americans. At the time, most white people believed that black people were inferior to whites. They thought they were lazy, stupid, and could not organize their lives, needing white people to instruct them. The variety of cunning means devised by fugitives to escape demonstrates how wrong this **stereotype** was.

African American men were first able to vote in 1867 in the Southern states – depicted here in *Harper's Weekly* – but the 15th Amendment was not passed until 1870.

BREAKING DOWN BARRIERS

The Underground Railroad brought slaves, free blacks, and white allies together in a common cause. They often worked together as equals and came to know each other. Many Underground Railroad activists held prejudices against black people even though they hated slavery. Although these prejudices continued to exist, working in the Underground Railroad helped to break down some of the barriers between the races.

HUMAN RIGHTS

The Underground Railroad can be seen as a movement for equal human rights in a society where white men alone had rights. Activists argued from a religious viewpoint that the law was morally wrong, so they had to break it to achieve justice. Angelina Grimke, who came from the South, became a Quaker and an abolitionist. In 1836, she appealed to Southern women to oppose slavery on religious grounds, arguing, "If a law commands me to sin I will break it".

▲ A demonstration for civil rights outside the Republican Party's national convention (large meeting) in Chicago, 1960.

THE LEGACY OF THE UNDERGROUND RAILROAD

The Underground Railroad was part of a longer struggle for equal rights. The amended laws after the Civil War did not bring equality for black people. States were able to make their own rules, and many states brought in laws to separate the races in all areas of public life, from schools to public transport and facilities. The situation for black people was worst in the South. In the following century, the **Civil Rights** movement of the 1960s challenged racial inequality and led to the Civil Rights Act of 1964, which made major forms of discrimination illegal.

MAKE YOUR CONTRIBUTION TO HISTORY

Research never ends. Why not try to find out some new or neglected facts about fugitive slaves and their descendants? Start your research in the history section of the public library or online. See pages 62–63 for some websites to help you get started.

WOMEN ABOLITIONISTS

In early to mid-19th century America, women were not allowed to speak in public, vote, or work in most professions. Although women were barred from taking part in "official" party politics, some black and white women joined the struggle against slavery. They played a major role in the Underground Railroad and set up women's anti-slavery societies. They gathered signatures on petitions to Congress and gave public lectures. Significantly, they linked the lack of slaves' rights to the absence of women's rights. Their abolitionist activities spurred them to fight for women's rights, too.

BECOME A PRIMARY SOURCE DETECTIVE

Set yourself a clear goal, for example, to find out more about the descendants of former slaves. Then do some background reading from secondary sources (written by historians) so that you understand the period of history you are investigating. Now look for primary-source evidence:

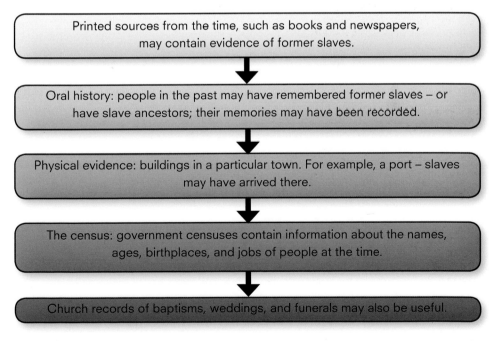

Printed sources from the time, such as books and newspapers, may contain evidence of former slaves.

Oral history: people in the past may have remembered former slaves – or have slave ancestors; their memories may have been recorded.

Physical evidence: buildings in a particular town. For example, a port – slaves may have arrived there.

The census: government censuses contain information about the names, ages, birthplaces, and jobs of people at the time.

Church records of baptisms, weddings, and funerals may also be useful.

Once you have discovered your evidence, think about it carefully. Where does it come from? Is a particular viewpoint being given? How reliable is the source? Then place your evidence in the context of the period, comparing it with other sources from that time.

TIMELINE

1705	Virginia's slave codes state that all non-white people can be enslaved and punished by masters as they wish; many states introduce similar codes
1793	The US government's Fugitive Slave Law requires all states to return fugitives to their owners; however, the law is widely ignored in the Northern states
Late 18th century	The Underground Railroad begins
1808	The United States bans the international slave trade
1820	The Missouri Compromise admits the new state of Missouri to the Union as a slave state, and Maine as a free state. It is a compromise between those who want new US states to allow slavery and those who believe new states should be free of slavery. Slavery is not permitted in the Northern states.
1840	Former slave Josiah Henson and others buy land in Canada to found Dawn, a settlement for fugitives
1841	A group of Kentuckians attack abolitionist John Rankin's home
1845–1846	Anti-black riots take place in Madison, Indiana
1846	Kentucky slave owners attack black people to try to stop the activities of the Underground Railroad
1850s	Stephen and Harriet Myers run the headquarters of the Albany, New York Underground Railroad from their home; former slave Harriet Tubman goes on several missions South to conduct fugitives to the North
1850	The Fugitive Slave Act makes it easier for slave owners to seize back fugitive slaves from anywhere in the US

1861–1865	The Civil War between the Northern and Southern states. The North wins; at least 623,000 soldiers die.
1865	The 13th Amendment to the US Constitution makes slavery illegal
1870	The 15th Amendment to the US Constitution allows all men to vote
1872	William Still's book, *The Underground Railroad: Authentic Narratives and First-Hand Accounts*, is published
1930s	The Works Progress Administration runs a major oral history project; the material is assembled as the 17-volume *Slave Narratives* in 1941
1954	Brown v. Board of Education ends segregation of the races in government-run schools
1960s	The Civil Rights movement challenges racial inequality
1964	The Civil Rights Act makes major forms of discrimination illegal
1990s	A federal programme is launched to identify and preserve sites linked to the Underground Railroad
2002	Archaeologists find evidence of Ramptown, a secret community of fugitive slaves in Michigan
2004	The Underground Railroad History Project buys the Stephen and Harriet Myers Residence to turn it into a museum
2009	The David Ruggles Center opens in Florence, Massachusetts
2012	The US National Park Service sponsors a national conference for the reunion of Black Seminoles, the descendants of fugitives who had settled with the Seminole American Indians

GLOSSARY

abolitionist person who fought to abolish slavery

amendment change that is made to a US law

artefact object that is made by a person, especially something of historical or cultural interest

brand use hot metal to mark the skin of a person or animal with letters or a symbol to identify them

cargo Underground Railroad term for escaped slaves being moved

census officially counting the country's population

Civil Rights campaign in the 1950s and 1960s to change the laws so that African Americans had the same rights as others

conductor person who helped to lead slaves to freedom

constitution system of laws and basic principles that govern a country

deeds legal document, especially one that proves ownership of a building

discrimination treating a particular group in society unfairly, for example because of their race or sex

foundry factory where metal or glass is melted and made into different shapes or objects

free black during slavery in the United States, an African American who was not a slave

fugitive person who is running away from somewhere and trying to avoid being caught

memoir account written by someone well known about their life

oral history collection and study of historical information through interviews with people who remember past events; in the past, interviews were written down but since the mid-20th century they have been recorded

pass document from a slave owner allowing a slave to make a journey

plantation large area of land where crops are grown; in the southern US states under slavery, growing sugar, cotton, and tobacco was common

preacher person who gives religious talks and often performs religious ceremonies, for example in a church

prejudice negative feelings towards a group of people that are not based on facts

Presbyterian type of Christian Protestant Church popular in the United States and which, in the North, took a stand against slavery

primary source document that contains information obtained by research or observation, not taken from other books

Quaker Christian religious group that meets without any formal ceremony, believes in doing community work, and in the 19th century, was strongly opposed to slavery

railroad American term for "railway"

refugee person who escapes to another country to seek safety from war, natural disaster, or bad treatment

runner person whose job is to pass on messages

secondary source book or other information source where the writer has taken the information from other sources and not collected it themselves

segregation policy of separating people of different races, religions, or sexes and treating them in a different way

station Underground Railroad term for a safe house where an escaped slave could shelter

station master Underground Railroad term for a person who sheltered escaped slaves, usually in their home

stereotype negative ideas about a whole group of people, which are not based on facts

steward person employed to manage a large house or other property

stockholder Underground Railroad term for a person who gave money to help escaped slaves

terminus Underground Railroad term for an endpoint of an Underground Railroad route, for example, in Canada

treason crime of doing something that could cause danger to your country

Vigilance Committee organization in the North set up by African Americans to protect fugitives from capture by slave hunters and prevent the kidnapping of free blacks to be sold into slavery

warrant legal document that is signed by a judge and gives the police authority to do something

wash-house in 19th-century America, a building for washing clothes

Works Progress Administration (WPA) US government programme (1935–1943) established to create millions of jobs for unemployed people

FIND OUT MORE

BOOKS

Non-fiction

Harriet Tubman (Real Lives), Deborah Chancellor (A&C Black, 2013)

Slavery and the Slave Trade (Research It!), Richard Spilsbury (Heinemann Library, 2010)

The Price of Freedom: How One Town Stood Up to Slavery, Dennis Brindell Fradin and Judith Bloom Fradin (Walker, 2013)

Fiction

Ghost Train to Freedom: An Adventure on the Underground Railroad, Faith Reese Martin (Life Reloaded Specialty Publishing, 2012)

Morning Star, Judith Plaxton (Second Story Press, 2011)

North by Night: A Story of the Underground Railroad, Katherine Ayres (Yearling, 2013)

Runaway! Dennis Maley (CreateSpace Independent Publishing Platform, 2011)

Unspoken: A Story from the Underground Railroad, Henry Cole (Scholastic, 2012)

WEBSITES

education.nationalgeographic.com/education/multimedia/interactive/did-you-know-the-underground-railroad/?ar_a=1

Basic information about the Underground Railroad, including an interactive journey, can be found on this National Geographic site.

www.freedomcenter.org/underground-railroad-0

The National Underground Railroad Freedom Center has a useful overview of the Underground Railroad and information about modern-day slavery.

johnparkerhouse.org

The John P. Parker Museum and Historical Society website has details about abolitionist John Parker and a clip from a film about him.

www.loc.gov/library/libarch-digital.html
The Library of Congress Digital Collections can be viewed online.

www.nps.gov/subjects/ugrr/education/upload/Junior-Ranger-Activity-Booklet.pdf
Try the activities in this booklet by the National Park Service about the Underground Railroad.

www.ohiohistorycentral.org/entry.php?rec=1518
Find out more about the people involved in the Underground Railroad in the border state of Ohio.

undergroundrailroadhistory.org
This website is about the activities of the Underground Railroad History Project, which researches and preserves the history of the Underground Railroad.

OTHER TOPICS TO RESEARCH

You might like to investigate the story of Harriet Tubman, who has become a legendary figure of the Underground Railroad.

You may also want to find about the abolitionist movement, which was fighting to end slavery in the United States. Key members of the movement were Quakers – you could investigate their role in the ending of slavery.

A parallel story is the struggle for women's rights in 19th-century America. Can you find out more about this topic?

PAGE 14 ANSWERS

1. Joe, I have two male fugitives and one mixed-race female fugitive at my house.
2. A large mixed-race Christian needs help; he will be in town on Tuesday afternoon and has $100 to pay his way.

INDEX